Badlands

CANADIAN
STARTERS

GLC 115 Nugget Avenue, Agincourt, Ontario M1S 3B1 (416) 291-2926

About Starters

Starters books are written and designed with young readers in mind. They are vocabulary controlled and the contents have been carefully checked by a critic reader and teacher panel.

Each book contains questions for teacher-directed learning, bright and simple illustrations, interesting and informative text, picture glossary and a table of facts.

ISBN 0-88874-404-8

Edited by: GLC Editorial Department
Illustrations: Henning Christensen Graphics
Critic Reader: Mrs. Margaret Knechtel, Reading Consultant,
Etobicoke Board of Education
Teacher Panel: Miss Grace Davis, Grade 2 Teacher,
John D. Parker Junior Public School,
Etobicoke Board of Education

Printed by: Ashton-Potter Limited
Film preparation: Graphic Litho-plate Inc.
Bound by: The Hunter Rose Company Ltd.

Printed and Bound in Canada

Uniquely Canadian Materials from GLC Publishers Limited
115 Nugget Avenue
Agincourt, Ontario

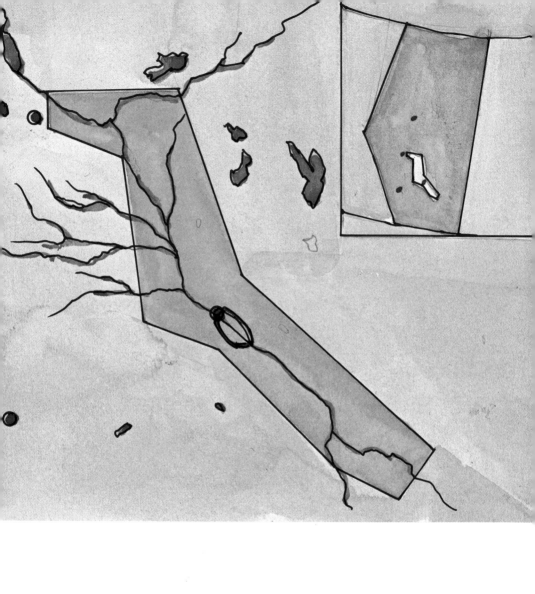

The badlands are in Alberta.

The badlands are a valley.

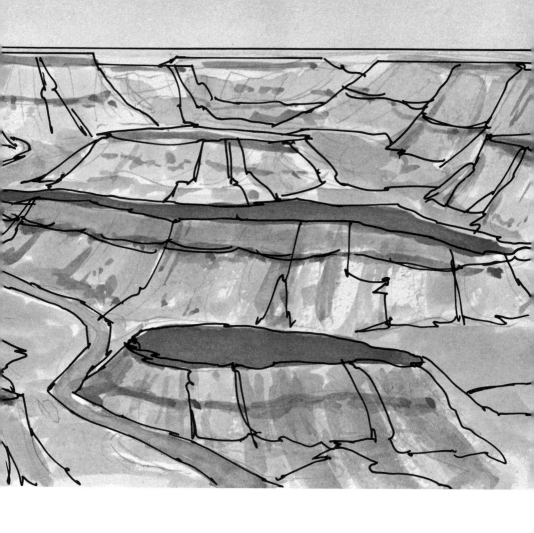

The Red Deer River flows through the valley.

The valley is dry and dusty.
It has very few flowers or plants.

There are many strange shapes in the valley.

butte

These hills are called buttes.

hoodoo

These rocks are called hoodoos.

Large dinosaurs lived in the badlands long ago.

8

The badlands were not dry and dusty long ago.

The swamp began to dry up.
The dinosaurs died.

After many years, the badlands were formed.

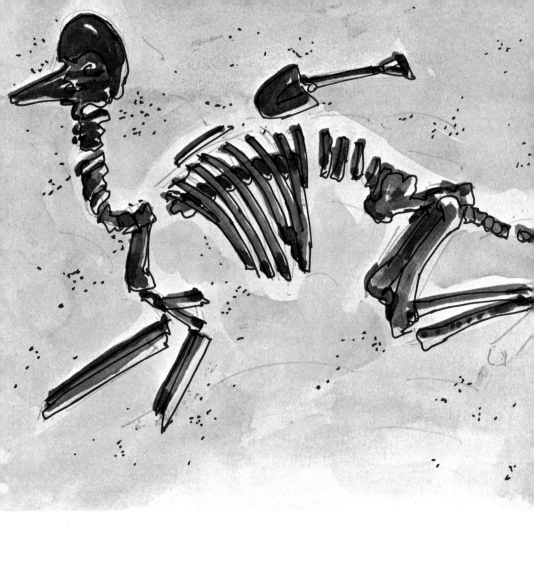

Today, the bones of dinosaurs are found
in the badlands.

12

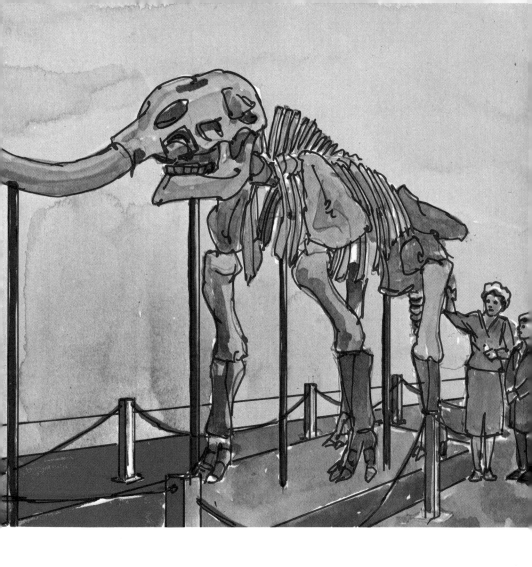

This dinosaur skeleton is in a museum.

There are many fossils in the badlands, too.

14

Fossils show plants and creatures from long ago.

The town of Drumheller is in the centre
of the badlands.

16

Tyrannosaurus Rex

There is a large dinosaur model in Drumheller.

Visitors drive along the Dinosaur Trail.

he Dinosaur Trail runs beside the Red Deer River.

The Dinosaur Trail crosses the river.
Cars cross on a small ferry.

There is a park on the trail.

It has many dinosaur models.

The badlands are sometimes called
the "Valley of the Dinosaurs."

22

The badlands help us to learn about
what it was like long ago.

PICTURE GLOSSARY

badlands
(page 1)

valley
(page 2)

butte
(page 6)

hoodoo
(page 7)

dinosaur
(page 8)

swamp
(page 10)

bones
(page 12)

skeleton
(page 13)

fossil
(page 14)

Dinosaur Trail
(page 18)

ferry
(page 20)

Dinosaur Park
(page 21)